THIS BOO
BELONGS TO :

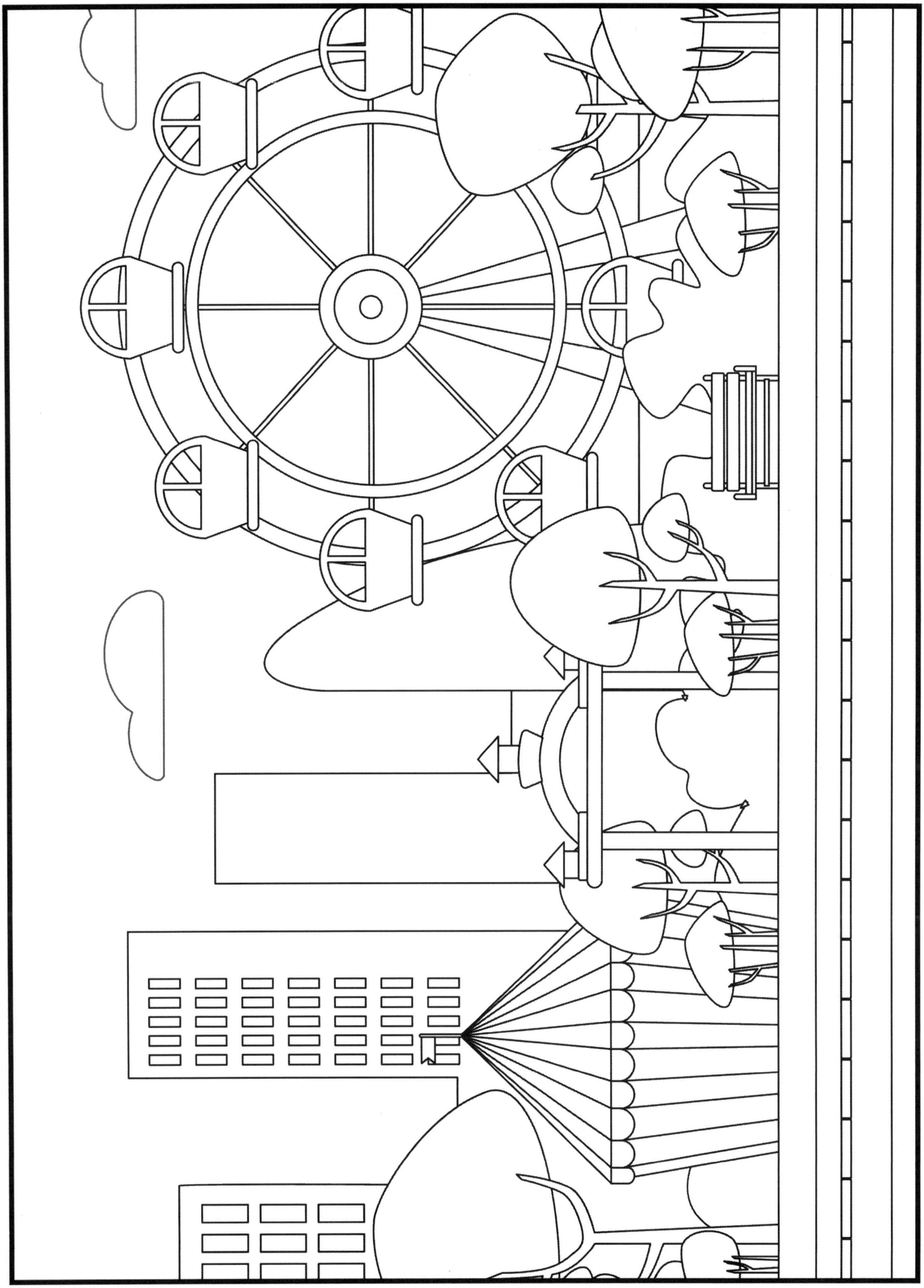

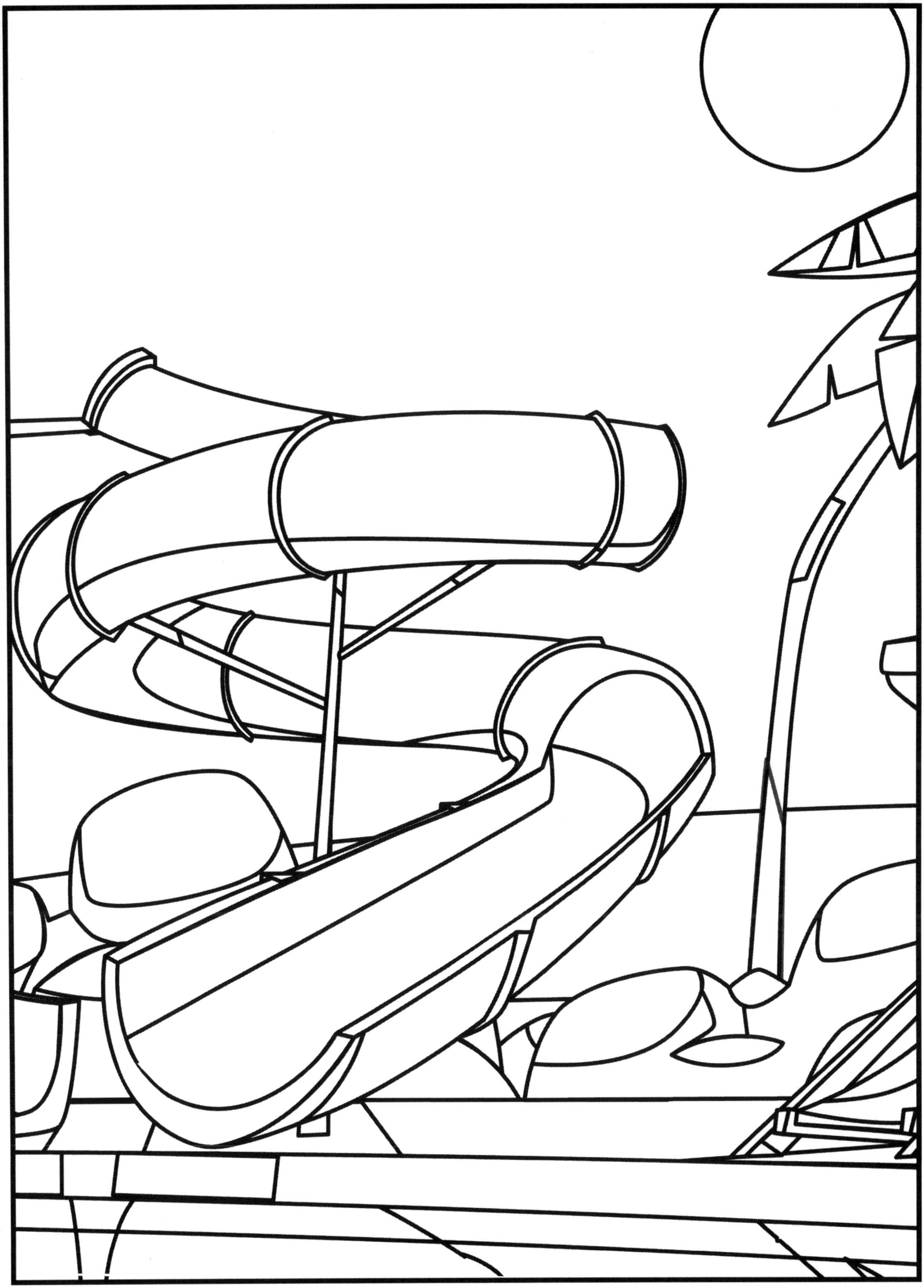

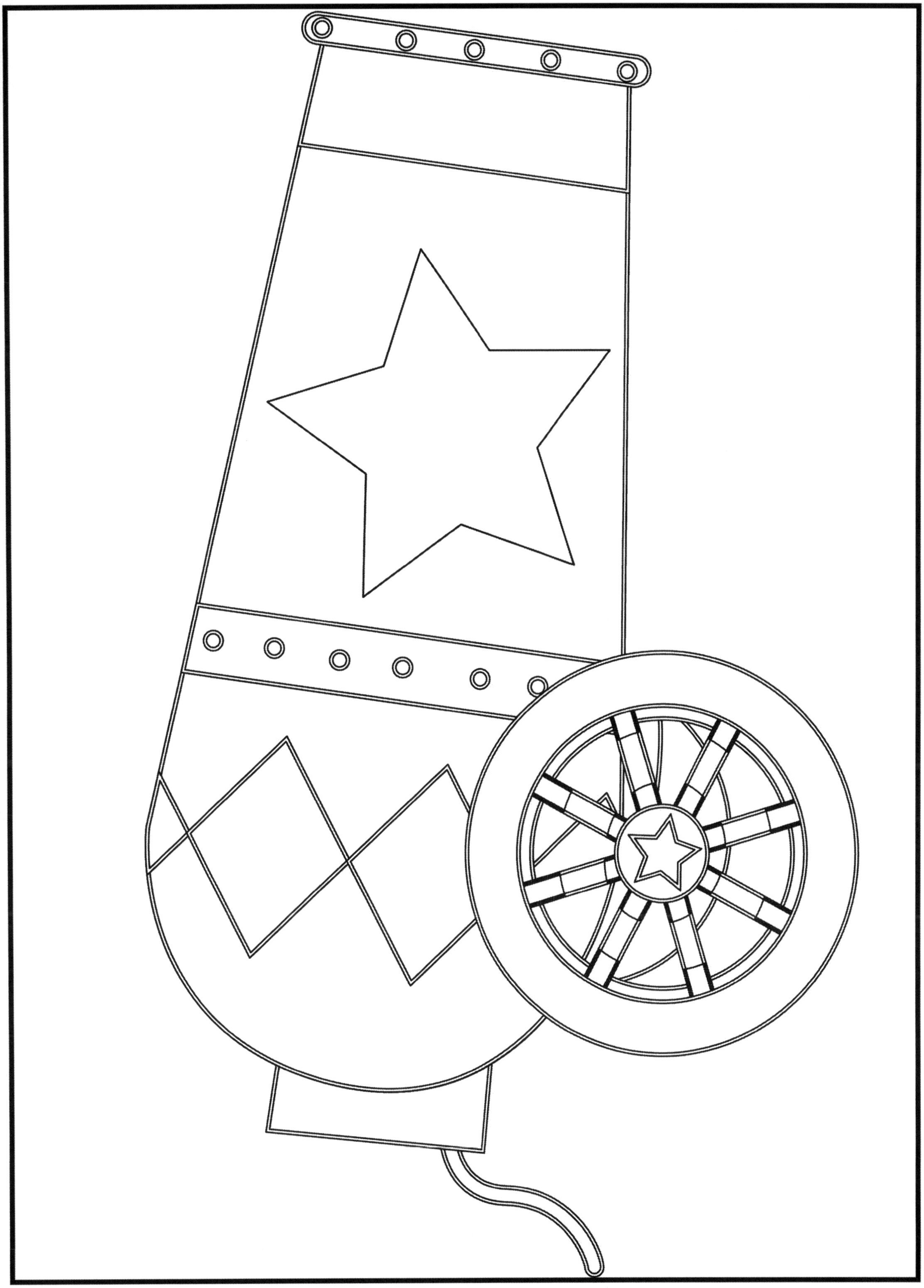

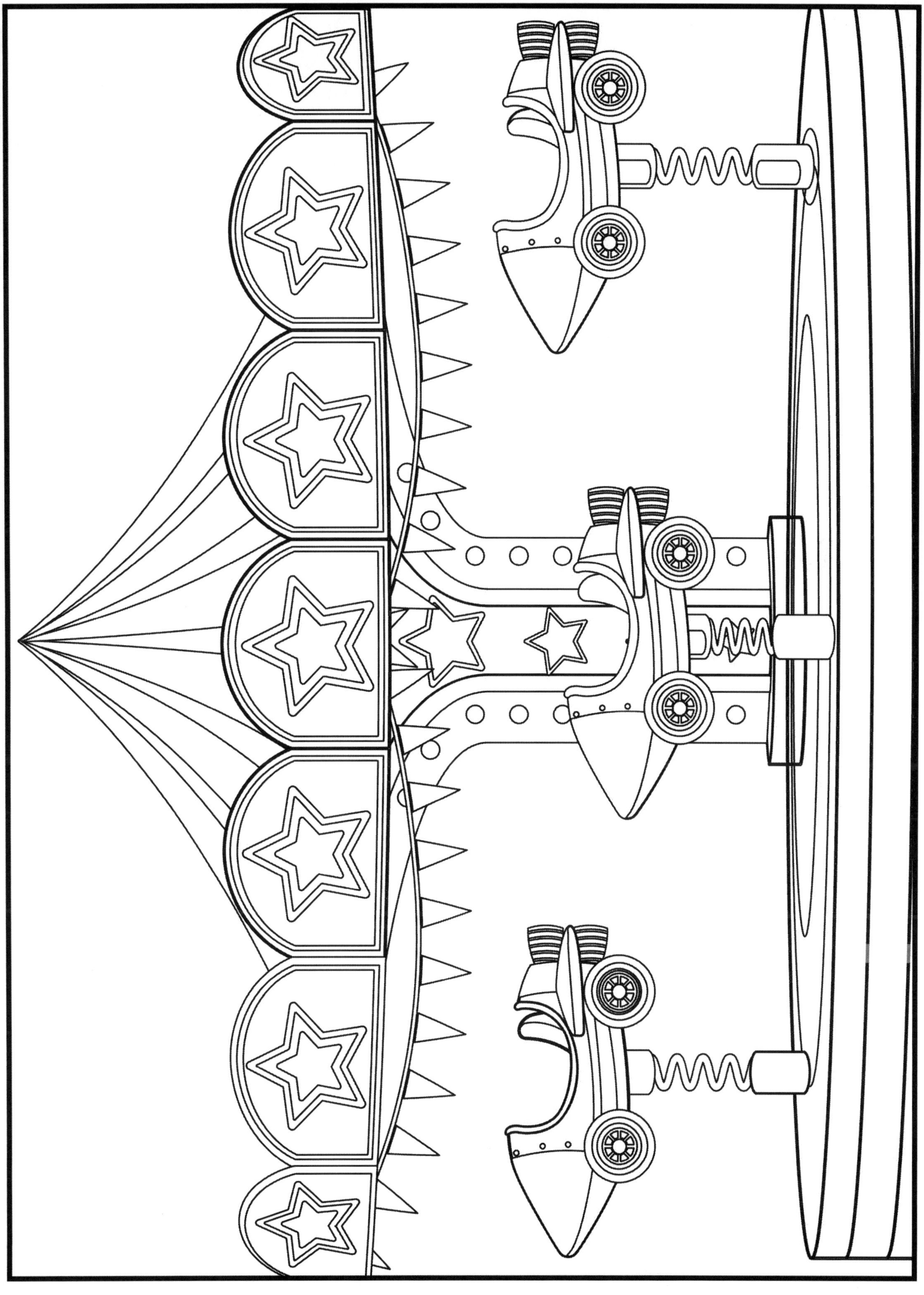

TICKETS

CIRCUS

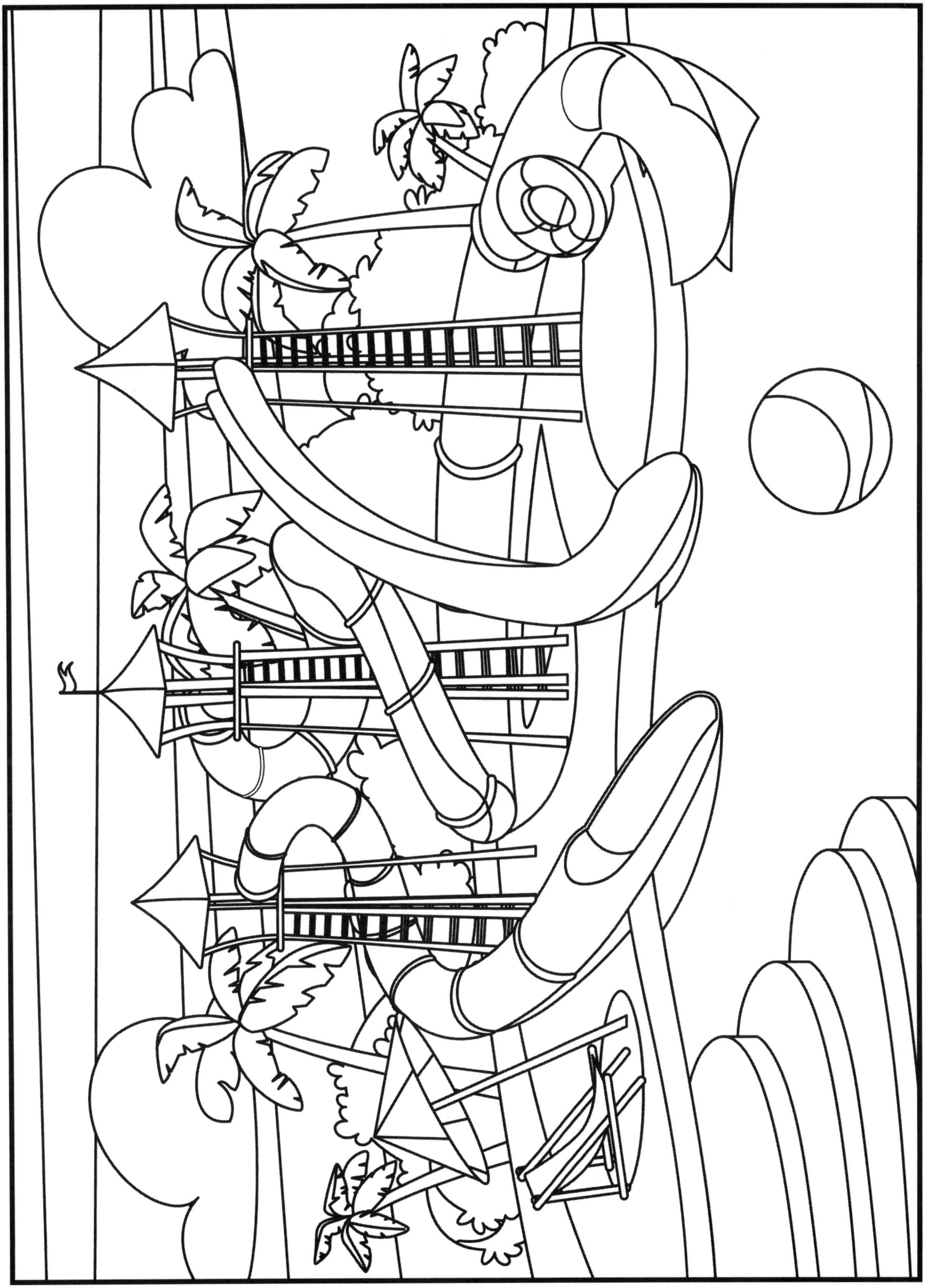

AMUSEMENT
PARK

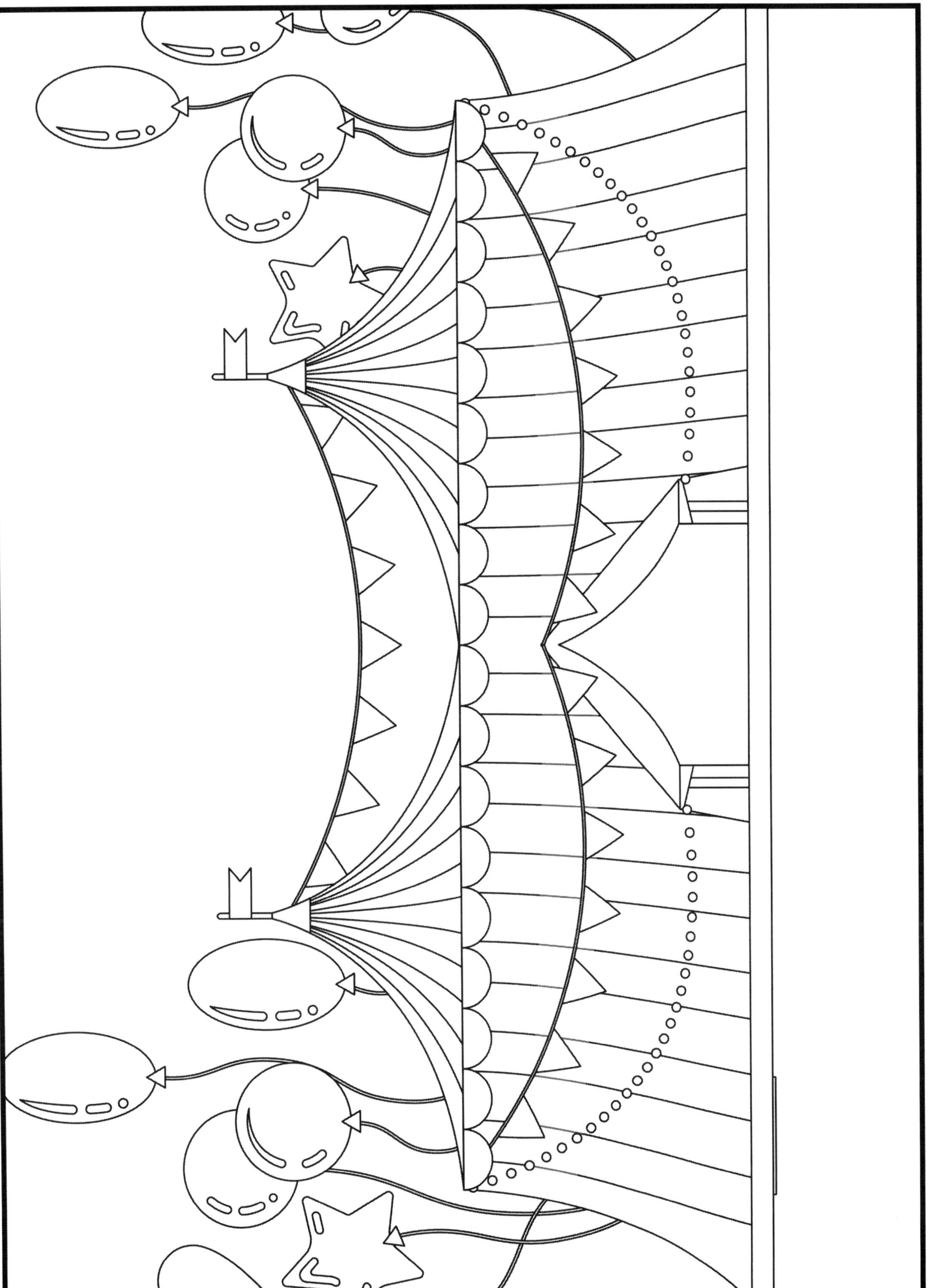

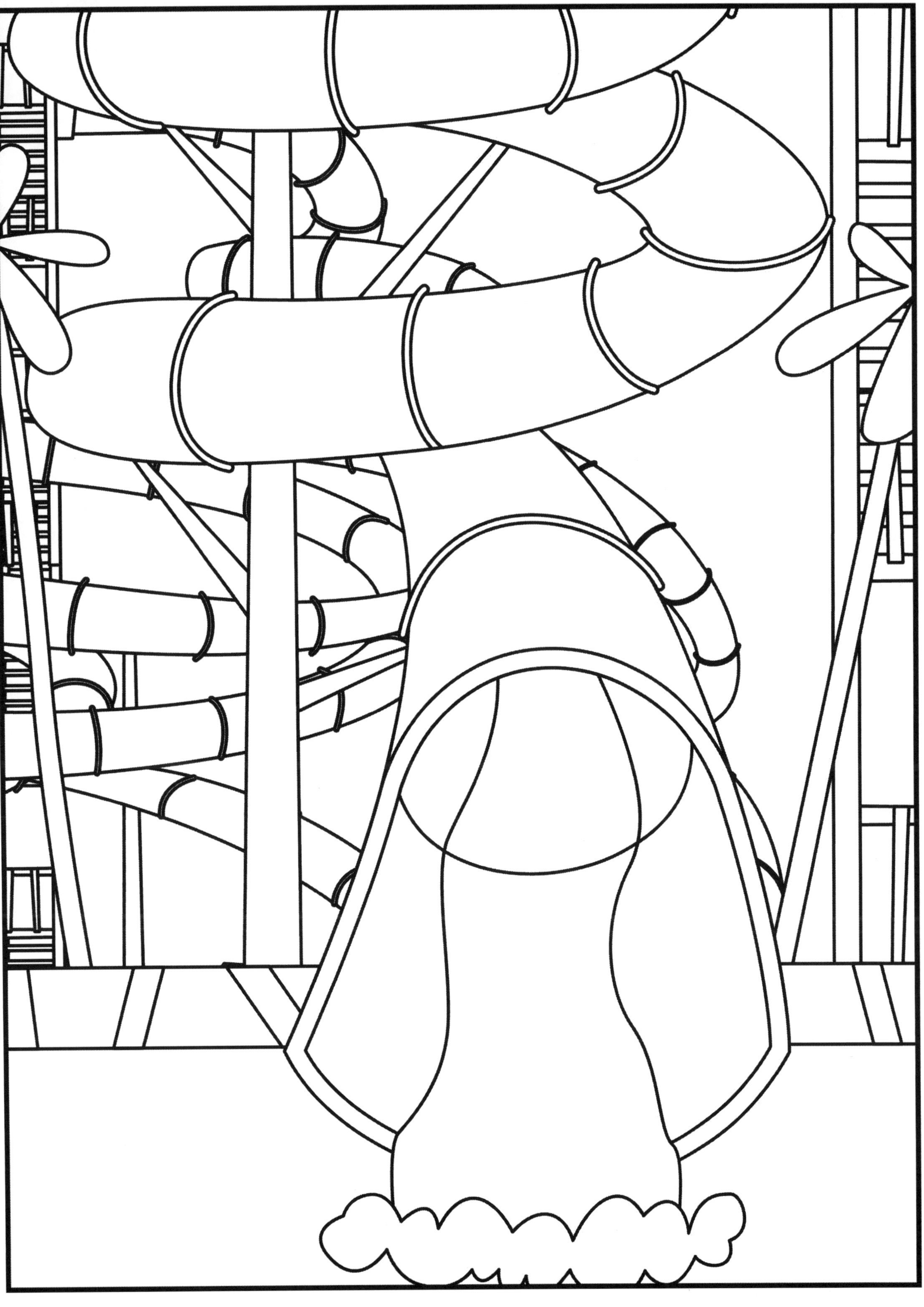

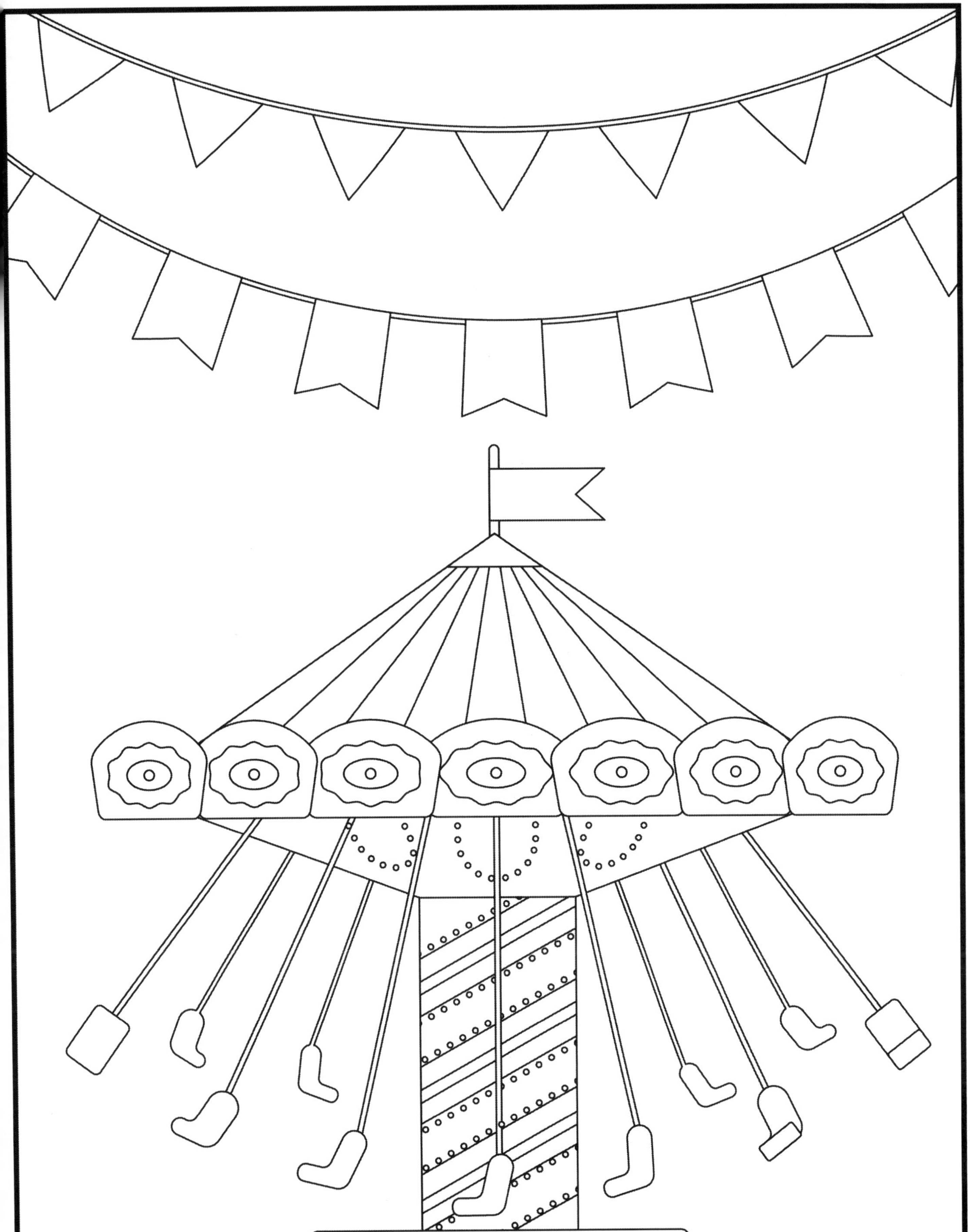

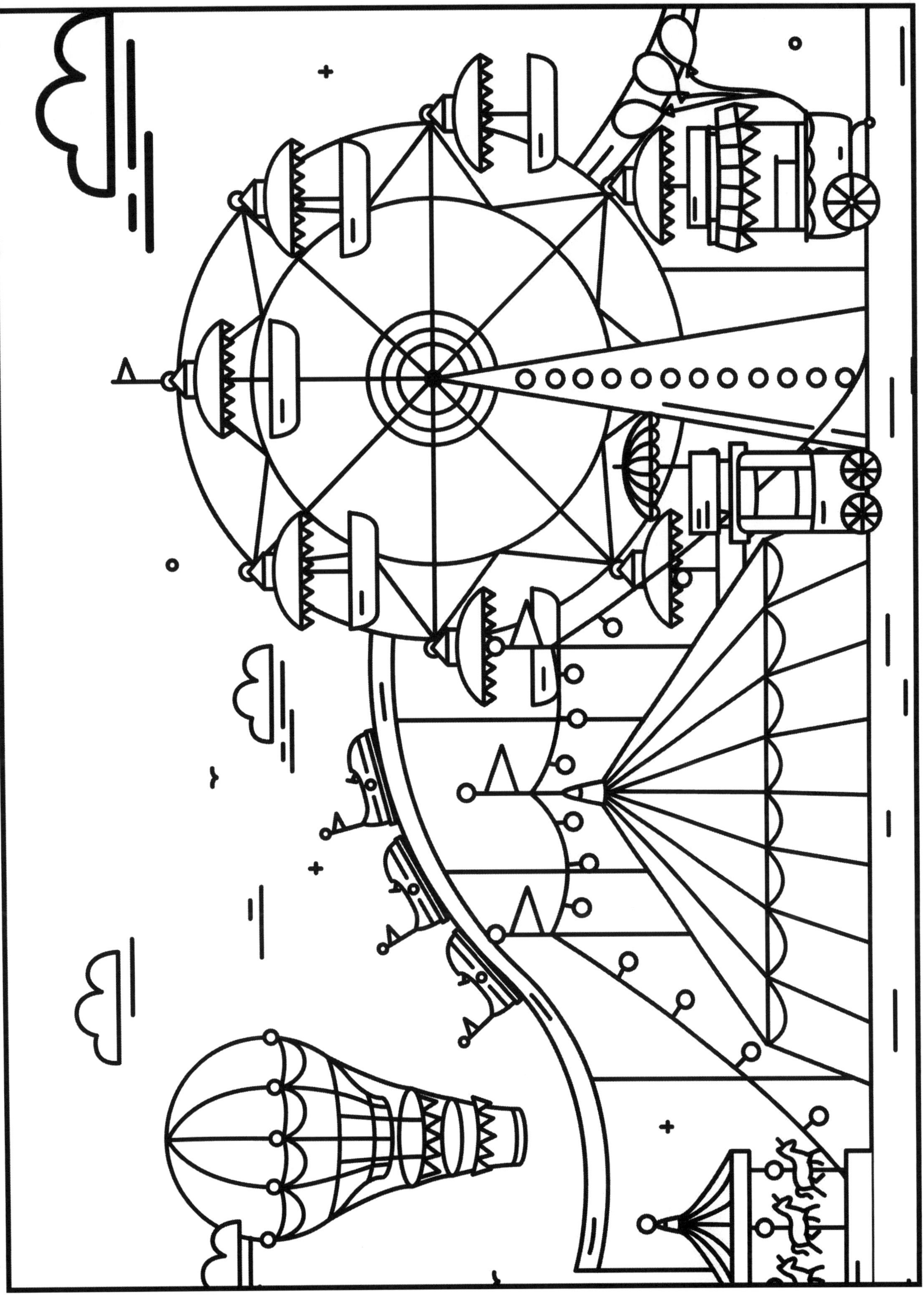

AMUSEMENT PARK

AQUAPARK

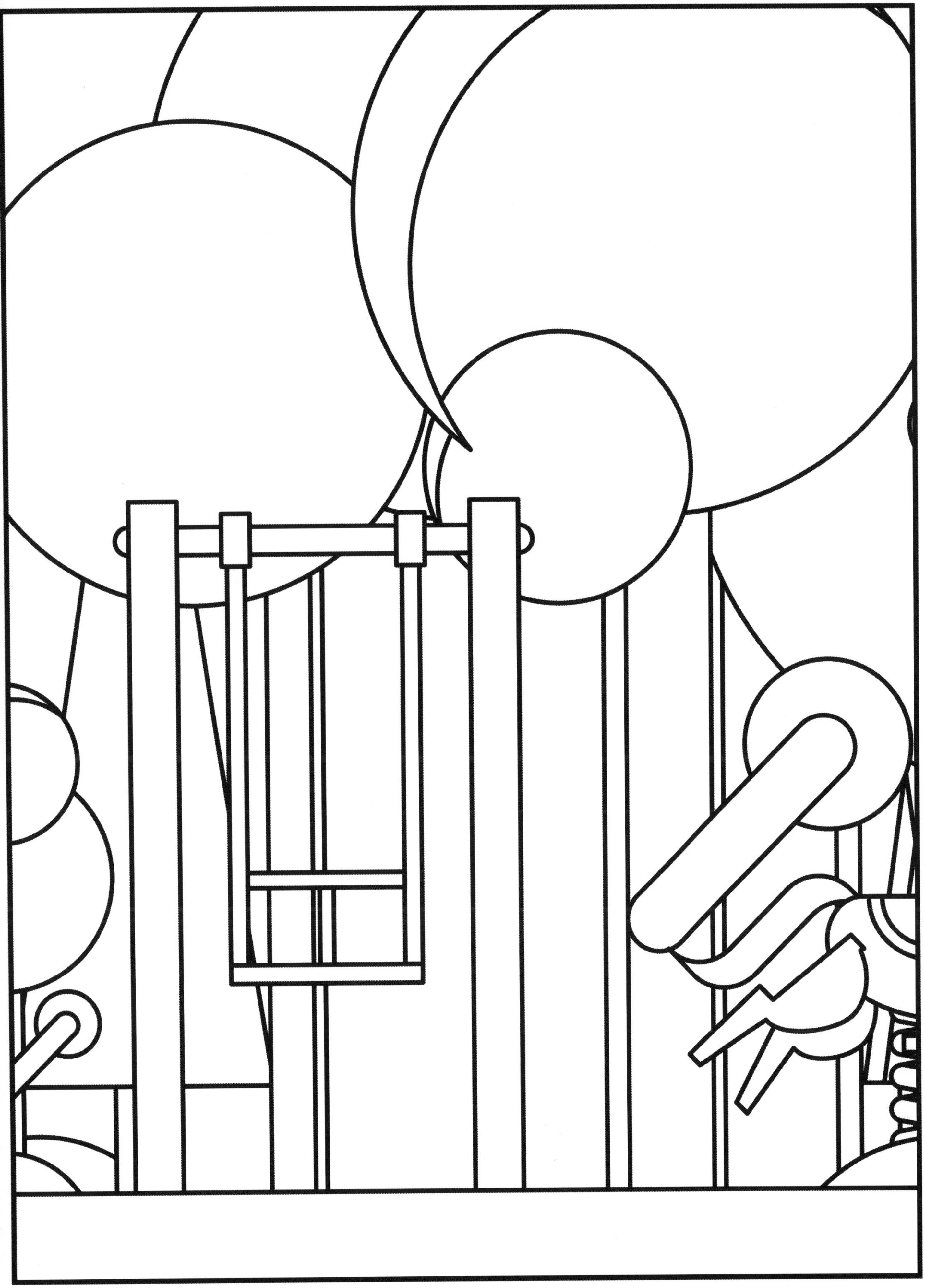

LAZY RIVER

GO!

Printed in Great Britain
by Amazon

64079585R00041